A Gift From Fadil

A Package Engineering Story

Written by the Engineering is Elementary Team

Illustrated by Keith Favazza

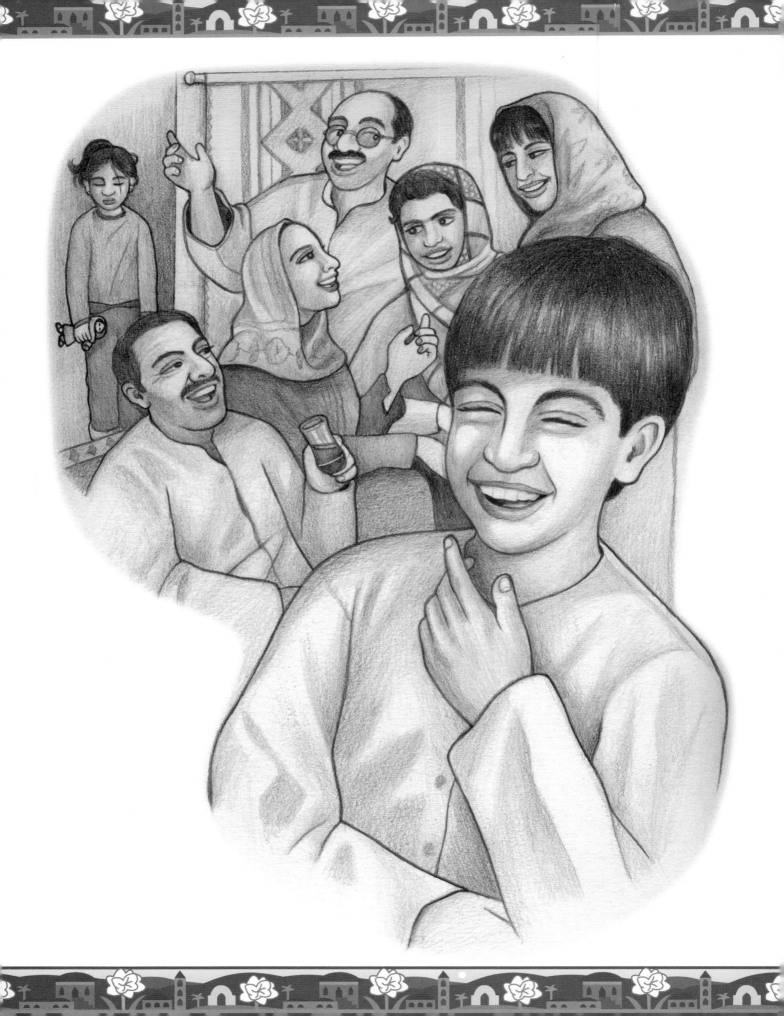

Chapter One | Wedding Worries

For the hundredth time that night, Fadil felt a laugh rising from his belly and blending with the laughter of his family. It was like this every time they got together and began telling stories. There was Mama's high-pitched laugh, Father's deep, booming laugh, and the laughs of all the aunts and uncles in between. Somehow all of the noise together formed a happy chorus.

The zing of excitement in the air made this gathering even more fun than usual. In less than a week, Fadil's big sister, Ikhlas, would be married to her fiancé, Jamal. Fadil had been to other 'urs parties for marriages, but because this celebration was for Ikhlas, he knew it would be extra special.

As the laughter died down to a lull, Uncle Hassan began

to tell the story of the day he and Aunt Rasha were married. *Oh, not this one again*, thought Fadil. Uncle Hassan was a great storyteller, but he did tend to tell the same ones over and over again. Fadil let his gaze wander across the faces of his family members. Father raised an eyebrow as he looked in Mama's direction, a signal they used any time Uncle Hassan began telling one of his favorite stories. Aunt Rasha leaned in toward Uncle Hassan and patted his hand, her dark eyes sparkling. Then Fadil's eyes settled on an empty seat. Where was Bashira?

Fadil hadn't noticed that his little sister, Bashira, had left the living room, but now he spotted her through the window, sitting in the yard on a small straw stool. She was frowning slightly. She looked . . . lonely, Fadil finally decided. And now that he thought about it, Bashira had been acting a bit strangely for the past few days.

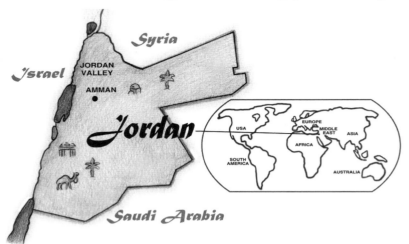

Fadil slipped outside into the warmth of the summer evening air. The daytime temperature had reached a sweltering 30 degrees Celsius in the Jordan Valley, where Fadil and his family lived. Once the sun

set, however, the air felt warm and comforting. He crossed
the yard and settled on the ground next to Bashira.

"Hey, there!" he said in his cheeriest voice. "You're
missing Uncle Hassan tell the story of his wedding day.
Never heard that one before, huh?" he joked, nudging her
with his elbow.

"Mmm-hmm," Bashira mumbled, her frown not
changing a bit.

Fadil studied Bashira's face, searching for an answer.
What could be the matter? Bashira stared into the distance.
Fadil tried to follow her gaze. She was looking through the

window into the living room. Framed by the warm glow of lamplight, Fadil could see Ikhlas smiling and chatting with Aunt Rasha. Ikhlas waved her hands around her head as she talked. *I bet she's talking about the* tahra *she'll wear over her hair during the ceremony,* Fadil thought. He'd heard that discussion almost as many times as Uncle Hassan's wedding story.

"Bashira," Fadil said, "are you upset about Ikhlas getting married?"

Bashira remained silent, but Fadil noticed her bottom lip beginning to shake.

"I . . . I . . ." Bashira began. "I feel so bad!" A few tears rolled down her cheek. "I know everyone is so excited about the wedding. Mama and Father and Ikhlas are so happy. But I don't want Ikhlas to get married."

Chapter Two | A Great Idea

Fadil looked at Bashira, concerned. "Come on," he said. "There's no reason to cry about it. Weddings are a lot of fun! First the sheikh will come, so Ikhlas and Jamal can sign their wedding contract. Then there will be the *'urs*, with food and dancing—and more food! You'll have a great time, you'll see."

"I understand why everyone is looking forward to the party," Bashira sputtered, as she gulped big breaths of air. "But what about after that? Once Ikhlas is married, she's moving away. And then she might forget us. Forget me."

Bashira was right that Ikhlas and Jamal would be moving. They'd both gotten jobs in Jordan's capital city, Amman, which was over 300 kilometers away.

"So that's why you've been so glum," Fadil said. As Bashira wiped away tears with the back of her hand, Fadil tried to think of something comforting to say. "There's no way Ikhlas will forget us. She'll still come visit us, and I bet we'll go visit her sometimes, too, all right?"

Bashira nodded her head, but tears kept streaming down her face. Fadil could tell she wasn't convinced.

Fadil bit his lip as he tried to think of something else to say. A soft breeze blew through the yard, rustling the amaryllis plants growing in pots next to the doorway of the house. The amaryllis were the pride of Mama's garden, with sturdy green stalks and milky white flowers. When Fadil was just a little boy, and Bashira an even littler girl, they would spend hours outside sitting by those flowers with Ikhlas as she read to them. Whenever he saw the amaryllis, Fadil thought of Ikhlas.

"Hey, I have an idea!" Fadil said. "What if we make

something special for Ikhlas to take with her? Something to remind her of us while she's in Amman."

Bashira looked up at him, her eyes a mix of sadness and curiosity. "Make her something? Like what?"

"What are some things that remind you of Ikhlas?" he asked.

Bashira thought. "Light blue, like the color of her head scarf," she began reluctantly. "*Kunafah*, because that's her favorite dessert. Reading . . . oh, and the amaryllis!" she said.

"That's exactly what I was thinking," Fadil said. "And I bet the amaryllis remind her of times she's spent with us. What if we dig up one of our amaryllis plants so Ikhlas can take it with her?"

"She could keep it at her new apartment!" Bashira said, clapping her hands. "It's perfect!"

"Great," Fadil said. "Tomorrow, we'll check with Mama. Then we'll get started."

"I want it to be a big surprise for Ikhlas and Jamal!" she squealed, then took off running toward the kitchen. *Big brother saves the day!* Fadil thought as he smiled to himself. He turned and looked down at the amaryllis. The pure white flowers seemed to glow in the moonlight. *So we'll probably just have to dig up an amaryllis and replant it in a pot*, Fadil thought. *How hard could it be?*

Chapter Three | Problem Solved?

The next morning, when Fadil walked into the kitchen, he could hear Bashira chattering to Mama in the yard explaining their idea. They were both standing just outside the kitchen door, Mama peeling vegetables and Bashira moving around excitedly. As Fadil joined them, Mama put down her knife and gave them both a tight hug. "That's a wonderful idea, my dear children," she said. "I'm sure Ikhlas will love it. You can use the gardening tools. And I think I have an old pot that might help you."

"Maybe I can decorate it!" Bashira said, smiling.

"Of course," Mama said. "Why don't you go explore the shed and let me know if there's anything else you need."

Bashira dashed across the yard. Fadil turned to follow.

When he reached the shed, he saw that a spade and a small rake had already been tossed outside. He heard a rustle, then a crash, then, "*Aiiee!*"

"Everything all right in there, Bashira?" Fadil asked.

"Great!" Bashira said, appearing in the doorway of the shed with a pot in one hand, a spade in the other, and a smear of soil across her forehead.

"Wow, we haven't even started yet and you already look like you've been rolling in dirt." Bashira wrinkled her nose at him, grabbed his hand, and tugged him toward the amaryllis.

"Now, which do you think looks like a good wedding gift?" Fadil asked.

"Hmm . . . I think this one looks good," Bashira said, pointing to an amaryllis plant with one large creamy blossom and two tight buds peeking out behind the flower petals. Bashira dropped to her knees and carefully began to dig around the base of the plant. Bashira lifted the amaryllis bulb and placed it gently in the terra-cotta pot she'd taken from the shed. As she began scooping dirt into the pot, she paused, a spade full of dirt hovering over the plant.

"I think we forgot something," Bashira said. "Ikhlas is moving right after she gets married. I don't want the plant to get crushed during all the moving and packing."

"We can put the plant in a box," Fadil said. "I have an old box in my room. Maybe you can decorate that, too."

A wave of satisfaction washed over Fadil. Bashira was feeling better and didn't seem to be as upset about Ikhlas's wedding. Problem solved!

Chapter Four | A Bump in the Road

Two days before the *'urs*, Bashira still seemed to be in bright spirits. Fadil had even seen her help Ikhlas try on her dress.

Bashira had told everyone who'd come to visit that she had a special gift she was going to give Ikhlas. She was especially excited to show Aunt Rasha the package they'd made.

Aunt Rasha worked with packages for her job. When he was younger, Fadil always thought this sounded funny. He'd imagined Aunt Rasha sitting at a desk, wrapping box after box in colorful paper, tying bows and ribbons onto packages. Eventually, Aunt Rasha had explained that she was a packaging engineer. Packaging engineers use their knowledge of science and math and their creativity to design packages for all types of objects. Aunt Rasha designed packages to transport certain types of food. This was important, because there aren't many areas in Jordan where crops can be grown. They do grow in the Jordan Valley, though. After a harvest, the fruits and vegetables need to be shipped from the valley to other parts of the country. Aunt Rasha's job was to design packages that protected the food so it arrived safely, without bruising.

After lunch, while the adults were sitting drinking tea, Bashira grabbed Fadil and Aunt Rasha and brought them outside to show off the package.

"Here it is!" Bashira said as she presented the transformed box. She'd covered the box with paper and had drawn hearts and stars all over it. On the front was a picture of Ikhlas and Jamal. *It actually looks really pretty*, Fadil thought.

"A few days ago, we dug up the plant, then I decorated the box, and then we put the plant inside," Bashira explained. "I even put in some cloth to fill the spaces in the box, so the flower wouldn't move around as much and get crushed." Aunt Rasha was nodding as Bashira spoke. But when Bashira lifted off the top of the box to show Aunt Rasha the plant, the nodding stopped. Fadil peered inside the box and saw the amaryllis plant, now shriveled and wilted.

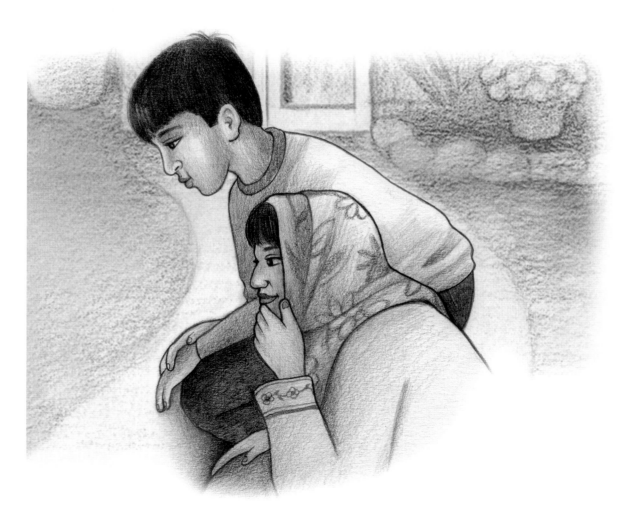

Bashira's bottom lip started to quiver, and Fadil's stomach dropped. He couldn't decide which looked sadder—the amaryllis or Bashira.

"Come now," Aunt Rasha said, in what Fadil recognized as her "calming" voice. It was the same soothing tone she'd used when he'd twisted his ankle playing football. "No need to be discouraged."

"The flower's dead," Bashira said between sniffles.

"No, no," Fadil said quickly, easing the plant out of the package. "I think it just needs some water. And maybe some time out of the box?" He hoped he sounded confident, but really he was scrambling for suggestions. *Why didn't I think about the plant needing water? Sunlight and air, too*, Fadil scolded himself. *Now I've ruined everything.*

"I think this plant should recover," Aunt Rasha said, lifting a sagging blossom with one finger to inspect it. "In the meantime, you can redesign your package."

Redesign? The whole thing was a failure, Fadil thought to himself. But he simply asked, "What do you mean, redesign?"

"This first design didn't work as well as you thought it would," Aunt Rasha said. "What you need to do now is improve your design. It's all part of the engineering design process."

"The engineering design process?" Bashira asked through her sniffles.

Aunt Rasha nodded. "I use it in my work all the time. The engineering design process is a series of steps you can use to help you solve a problem. The first step is to ask good questions."

"Like, why didn't this package work?" Fadil asked.

"Well, sure," Aunt Rasha said. "You want to ask questions that will make the criteria—the standards for your package—clear. You might ask what this plant needs to stay healthy, even when it's inside the package."

Bashira wiped a few tears off her cheek with the back of her hand. "We learned about plants and flowers in school," she said. "The leaves need energy from sunlight to help the plant grow and make food. The roots need water and nutrients from the soil to keep the plant healthy. Then the stem moves the water and nutrients to all the different plant parts."

"Very good!" Aunt Rasha said. "Packaging engineers need to think about both the object or product that will be inside the package, and what the package needs to do. Your object, the amaryllis plant, has leaves, roots, stems, and flowers. Some of these parts are more delicate than others, and your package needs to protect those parts. But your package also needs to look like a beautiful wedding present and display the flower."

"Right!" Bashira agreed.

"Then you need to look at the materials you have available to make the package. How can they be used or changed to meet the needs of what you're packaging? The next step is to imagine some package designs that will meet the needs of the plant and the package. Then you can make a plan for one design and create it. After you test it out, you can improve your technology and start the whole process again."

"Technology?" Fadil asked. "Do you think the package needs electricity to work?"

"Technology doesn't always use electricity," Aunt Rasha explained. "I like to think of technology as any thing, system, or process designed to help you solve a problem."

"We can't give Ikhlas the plant like this!" Bashira said. "Our package needs to solve the problem of keeping the plant healthy."

"Right," Fadil said. "With the engineering design process, I think we'll be able to come up with a great technology to keep the plant safe and healthy. We just need to improve our ideas." As he said this aloud, he felt better, too.

"I have an idea that might inspire you," Aunt Rasha said. "Come on, we're going on a trip!"

Chapter Five | A Trip to the *Souq*

Aunt Rasha led them to the *souq*. Fadil and Bashira had spent many hours there, talking to vendors and wandering through the rows. Their neighbor Ebrahim owned one of the stands. Aunt Rasha's orange skirt was like a bright banner as she wove between the carts. Suddenly she stopped in front of a cart selling eggs and vegetables. The vegetables were stacked high, like miniature mountains. "Look at this packaging," she said, touching the molded cardboard in between each layer of eggs, cradling them like jewels. "Why do you think these eggs are packaged differently than, say, the cucumbers?"

Fadil could feel Bashira's eyes on him. Her forehead was furrowed quizzically. Fadil examined the cucumbers.

They were just stacked one on top of the other in a box. "Well," Fadil began, "maybe they're packaged differently because they're very different products. Eggs have fragile shells," he said. Aunt Rasha gave him an encouraging nod. "Once the shells are broken," he continued, "the egg inside can't be used. They need to be protected by something—like the cardboard." Fadil paused to think a moment.

Bashira perked up. "Cucumbers are hard and strong, right? They don't need as much protection, so they don't need to be snuggled in cardboard."

Aunt Rasha applauded. "Exactly," she said. "Packages need to protect and preserve the objects inside them. But the best way to protect and preserve something can depend on the object itself. The cucumbers don't need as much protection. In fact, if they were cushioned as much as the eggs, we would call that overpackaging. If you overpackage a product, you waste materials and money. Now let's think about something different," she said, turning away. Fadil grabbed Bashira's hand and scrambled to keep up with his aunt. They stopped in front of a cart holding ceramic plates and cups, each piece inside its own box with paper wrapped around it.

"Now, how about these objects?" Aunt Rasha asked. "How might they need to be packaged?"

"These cups are breakable!" Bashira said. "I know, because I broke one of Mama's." She blushed.

"That must be why each one of these pieces is packed on its own, with paper for cushioning in between," Fadil said. "That way, when they bounce around on the way to the *souq*, they won't break."

"Right again," Aunt Rasha said. "Now," she said, tapping her chin as she stood on her tiptoes to look around the *souq*, "I think we need to make just one more stop." She led Fadil and Bashira to another stall. "Here we are.

The perfume seller." Fadil recognized the brand that Mama wore on special occasions. "What do you notice about these packages?" Aunt Rasha asked.

"They're all different," Bashira said. "But the packages are all pretty little boxes."

"And what is on the boxes?" Aunt Rasha asked.

"They all have writing on them," Fadil said. "And they're all different colors. They look . . ."

"Fancy?" Bashira suggested.

"Yeah," Fadil said, nodding approvingly. "And expensive, too. These packages don't just hold the bottles. They also tell us something about what's inside."

"What a smart niece and nephew I have," Aunt Rasha said, pulling them close. "All sorts of packages can contain products. For each product, packaging engineers need to think about the type of package that will be the best fit for what's inside. Sometimes it might be most important to protect and preserve the object the package will contain. Other times, we need to communicate with the customer using writing or pictures. And sometimes, we need to make sure to display a certain feeling with the package, to show that the object inside is special and beautiful."

"You know, there are really two packages for each perfume," Fadil said. "There's the box on the outside and the bottle holding the perfume on the inside."

Contain, protect, preserve, communicate, and display. The words floated through Fadil's head. *We'll need to make sure our amaryllis package does all of those things.*

"So now that you've thought about these things, do you think you can use the engineering design process to redesign your package?" Aunt Rasha asked.

Chapter Six | Creative Thinking

An hour later, Fadil and Bashira sat on the floor surrounded by crayons, scissors, and paper. As he looked at the materials, Fadil admitted to himself that he wasn't exactly sure how they would improve their plant package. After all the things they'd talked about with Aunt Rasha, and all the packages they'd looked at in the *souq*, could they really create something that worked?

"Fadil, the *'urs* is only two days away," Bashira said. "Do you think we can do it?" Fadil could see the nervousness in her dark eyes, and he knew they *had* to succeed.

Fadil smiled with new resolve. "Do I think we can do it? I *know* we can. We'll just use the engineering design process that Aunt Rasha told us about as a guide. Do you remember the first step she mentioned?" he asked.

"I think I do. Asking good questions?" Bashira asked.

"That's right," Fadil said. "And we've already started asking questions about what the plant needs. Remember everything you told me this morning about how to take care of plants?" Bashira nodded proudly. "Well, now we have to imagine ways to create a package for the plant that will let the plant get all the things it needs—like air and water and sunlight."

"But how will we do that?" Bashira fired back. "We'll have to make sure the plant can get water while it's inside the box."

"You're right," Fadil said. "And sunlight will need to get to the plant, too. What if we tried something like this?" Fadil sketched a box on a piece of paper. "There," he said, holding the paper up. "I think this is part of the imagine step that Aunt Rasha talked about."

"I like that," Bashira said, looking at Fadil's sketch. "It looks like it would work. It's a lot more open than the other package we used. Maybe we don't need to put so much cloth around the bulb of the flower, either. That part of the plant is pretty tough."

"Right," Fadil said. "Maybe we overpackaged our last

design a bit. And I think we could use fewer materials on the outside, too. If we cut the materials correctly, I bet we could even use the leftover pieces to support the stem inside the package!"

"I see what you mean!" Bashira said, the excitement returning to her voice.

"Maybe you could imagine some package designs, too," he suggested. "Then we can pick the one we like best to really plan."

Bashira grabbed a crayon and started drawing, her eyes squinting in concentration. It took the rest of the afternoon for Fadil and Bashira to choose one of the designs they'd imagined together, make a plan, and create their package. Finally they sat looking at the amaryllis, now placed in their redesigned box.

"So, you know what we have to do now?" Fadil asked. Bashira looked up at him, questioning. "We have to test it! We'll see how the plant does in the package overnight, and then tomorrow we can make improvements if we need to. Then our package design should be all set for the *'urs*!"

Chapter Seven | The Big Day

Early on the morning of the *'urs*, before the sun had risen, Fadil awoke. He leapt out of bed and joined his family in the living room, just in time for the first *salat* of the day. Fadil bowed toward the floor, his forehead resting on the fine woven threads of the *sajjada*. He knew that today's prayers were extra special because of the celebration that was almost here. Fadil couldn't help thinking about what a great big sister Ikhlas had been to him. *I hope Bashira feels I've been half as great a big brother to her*, he thought.

....

After Friday prayers, Fadil sat in the living room with his family, excitedly waiting for Jamal and his family to arrive. Bashira's eyes glittered like stars as she sat next to

Ikhlas, admiring her wedding garb. When she noticed Fadil looking at her, she leaned in and whispered, "Can I show her now?" Fadil grinned and shook his head no.

"We should show the package to Ikhlas and Jamal together. Just wait a bit," he said.

Fadil's ears perked up as he heard footsteps outside. A rumble of excitement spread through the room—Jamal and his family had arrived with the sheikh! While the women from both families stayed indoors, Fadil and the other men went outside to wait while the sheikh prepared the marriage contract. After Jamal signed the contract, the sheikh brought it inside to Ikhlas.

Everyone gathered together to walk to Jamal's parents' house, where the real party would begin. As Fadil watched Bashira skipping ahead of him, her arms fluttering like the wings of a hummingbird, he knew that her worries about Ikhlas getting married had melted away. He couldn't help wondering if she was more excited about the wedding, or about the present she would give Ikhlas and Jamal later!

Chapter Eight | Presenting the Present

Sitting with Father and Uncle Hassan, Fadil devoured plate after plate of *mansaf*. He was so full he thought he would burst, but he did manage to finish off some *kunafah* for dessert, too. Then the dancing began—outside for the men, inside the house for the women. Fadil couldn't help wondering if Bashira had already revealed the surprise package. He wouldn't know until the end of the night, when his family would say goodbye to Ikhlas.

As the sky grew darker and bright stars began to appear like pinpricks overhead, guests began to leave. Eventually all the women from Fadil's family came outdoors. As soon as Bashira spotted Fadil, she ran to his side, clutching the package behind her back. "Can I show them now?" Bashira asked.

Fadil smiled and nodded, then followed her toward Ikhlas and Jamal. Fadil was surprised at the flutter in his stomach. Was he nervous? He and Bashira had put a lot of effort into this project. Maybe he was a bit anxious about what Ikhlas and Jamal would think.

Bashira held the amaryllis package protectively behind her back and began to tell Ikhlas and Jamal the story of the package. "At first," she said, "I was worried that when you got married, you might forget all of us back home. But Fadil reminded me that we'll always be connected. Aunt Rasha

helped us make something for you—a reminder of us that you can bring to your new house."

With that, she brought the package from behind her back and held it out. Ikhlas carefully took the package. "Oh! It's one of the amaryllis," she said. "It's perfect." Fadil thought he saw her eyes glistening and he felt a tightening in his throat, too. Ikhlas knelt down and gave Bashira a hug, then turned to Fadil. "Fadil, thank you so much," she said as she wrapped her arm around his shoulders.

Chapter Nine | Ideas in Bloom

At the end of the evening, Fadil stood with Aunt Rasha and Uncle Hassan.

"I'm so proud of you and your sister," Aunt Rasha said.

"I was very impressed," Uncle Hassan added.

"Fadil!" a voice called from the house. As he turned, Fadil saw their neighbor Ebrahim heading toward him.

"I noticed you and Bashira giving that amaryllis flower to Ikhlas," Ebrahim said. "Seeing all that work you did gave me an idea. Do you think you'd want to make more of those for me? Maybe even sell the flowers and packages at the *souq*? I'll give you a good share of the profits."

Fadil raised his eyebrows in surprise. "Really?" he asked. "You think the amaryllis would sell?"

"I do." Ebrahim nodded his head. "It's a great package for selling flowers. Think about it: the customers can see the amaryllis inside, and I can care for them easily because of the openings you made in the package. Plus, the instructions you wrote on the package are very helpful."

Aunt Rasha smiled and nodded encouragingly. "What a wonderful idea!" she said. "Fadil, the package engineering you and Bashira did was wonderful. We could test this package by counting how many flowers we sell, and then do some more research."

"Like asking customers what they think?" Fadil asked.

Aunt Rasha nodded.

"Yeah, that could work," Fadil said, thinking out loud. "We could make lots of improvements based on what the customers say. Maybe even change the materials we're using."

Aunt Rasha reached out and ruffled Fadil's hair. "I can see those ideas blooming already!"

Design a Package

The next time you give someone a present, don't just wrap it or decorate it with a bow—design the package so it's a perfect match for the present inside!

Materials

- ☐ Cardboard
- ☐ Tape
- ☐ Scissors
- ☐ Ruler
- ☐ Markers or crayons
- ☐ Packages from around your home
- ☐ A gift to package

Ask About the Gift You're Giving

Is the gift you're giving fragile? What is it made of? Is it big or small? Is it alive, like the plant Fadil gave his sister? Your final package design will depend a lot on what you are packaging. You'll also have to think about whether your package will be mailed. Will the package have to last for a long time, or will it be thrown away once the present has been opened? You might want to create a list of all the things you need your package to do.

Imagine Lots of Designs

Now that you've listed all the requirements for your package, imagine different designs. Could you recycle any old packages from your home and reuse them to create your new package design? After you've asked good questions and imagined lots of possible designs, it's time to pick one, plan it out carefully, and create it!

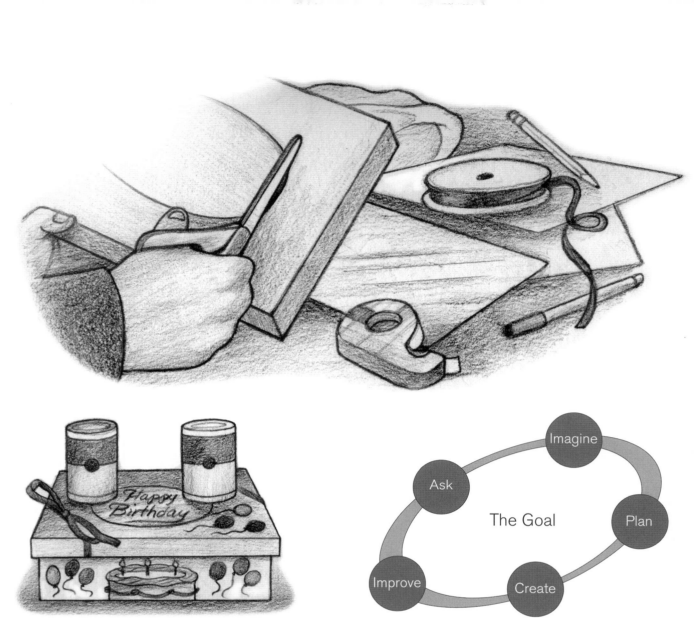

Plan and Create Your Package

Plan your package design by making a drawing before you begin construction. Once you have a plan that you like, create your package design. You may want to test your package design before you put your gift inside. If one of the requirements for your package is that it's strong, for example, you might want to place a few soup cans on top of it to be sure it doesn't buckle under weight.

Improve Your Package Design

Use the engineering design process to improve your package design. Use the Internet or go to the library to learn more about the field of package engineering. Can you use fewer materials or use only recycled materials to make your package better?

Glossary

Aiee: Jordanian term for "whoops." Pronounced *eye.*

Amaryllis: A plant with large flower blossoms that blooms every year.

Engineer: A person who uses his or her creativity and understanding of mathematics and science to design things that solve problems.

Engineering design process: The steps that engineers use to design something to solve a problem.

Kunafah: A dessert made from pastry, sweet cheese, and syrup. Pronounced *KOO-nah-fah.*

Mansaf: A Jordanian dish made from lamb, rice, and yogurt. Pronounced *MAN-sahf.*

Packaging engineer: An engineer who designs packages for many different types of objects. Packages have different functions, such as containing, preserving, protecting, displaying, and communicating information about what's inside.

Sajjada: A mat used during Muslim prayer. Pronounced *sah-HAHD-ah.*

Salat: A Muslim ritual prayer, performed five times throughout the day. Prounounced *suh-LAHT.*

Sheikh: An Arab religious leader. Pronounced *shake*.

Souq: Jordanian word for a traditional market or bazaar. Pronounced *sook*.

Tahra: Jordanian word for a wedding veil. Pronounced *TAH-ra*.

Technology: Any thing, system, or process that people create and use to solve a problem.

'Urs: Casual term used to describe the feasting and celebrating after a marriage ceremony. Pronounced *ers*.